THE GARDEN LIBERATED

Paolo Pejrone

THE GARDEN LIBERATED

An Evolution of Italian Garden Design

Edited by Alberto Fusari · Photographs by Dario Fusaro

New York · Paris · London · Milan

All of the photographs included in this book represent parts of projects executed over time based on an idea by the architect Paolo Pejrone; for the projects depicted from p. 26 to p. 151, he was also assisted by the architectural firm of Franco Brugo of Revello, who signed these projects with him.

Contents

6   Introduction

13   **THE GARDENS**

14   **A Garden Whose Leaves Are Strong
and Robust, but Not Enough**
Garden of Leaves, Castello di Racconigi (Turin)

26   **A Renewed Garden**
Garden in the Hills of Turin

44   **Of Shears and Imagination**
Garden in the Countryside of Capalbio (Grosseto)

58   **Glorious Acclimatizations
from the Past and New Prospects**
Villa della Pergola, Alassio (Savona)

76   **An Ecosystem Rediscovered**
Garden in Lazio

94   **A Vegetable Garden with Flowers**
Locanda Rossa, Capalbio (Grosseto)

106   **An Agricultural and Happy Capri**
Garden in Capri (Naples)

124   **Simple and Sophisticated**
Garden in Bolgheri (Livorno)

138   **Plant Minimalisms**
Garden in the Hills of Bologna

152   **Repairs**
Colle dell'Infinito, Recanati (Macerata)

170   **A Lagoonal Triumph**
Royal Gardens, Venice

185   **WHETHER INDIGENOUS OR NOT, CULTIVATING AND
TESTING ARE PART AND PARCEL OF THE GAME**

Introduction

Paolo Pejrone

Once upon a time there was a young landscapist who might find it hard to recognize himself now, worn by all these years of work and more and more convinced that simplicity is the best solution. He would probably turn up his nose at what he sees, because at the beginning one wants to distinguish oneself and thus tends to complicate things: plants and designs are his signature style and the more special they are, the more valuable they are. My first gardens were rather close-knit: growth was expected, of course, but then they had to be kept in check, according to the plan, respectful of the composition, of the sought after and at times delicate balance between forms and botany. They lasted for as long as they lasted, for as long as someone did what they could to maintain them as they were. Some disappeared, and others survived, at least their skeletal structure did, spare and free from redundance.

Over time I realized the garden is something much bigger than the original idea, the scene, whether big or small, that we garden designers imagine, something that expands and changes, just as the relationship with the person who owns or cultivates it changes. The garden is a process, an engine of sorts, and all we do is get it started and keep an eye on it. It would be useless and pointless to try to block it, crystallize it, not let it evolve according to its own motion. In that case it would become none other than an ornament, and besides that ephemeral and totally dependent on human care. Today, whenever I think of a new garden, I always try to take into account, in the most realistic and honest way possible, this "breath," this dilation that every single element will encounter, the slow growth, the growth that is less slow, and the very fast growth, the disappearances, how the relationship between light and shadow will be overturned, how the roots will conquer space. This explains why the gardens of my mature years—the ones we shall "stroll through" in this book—are rather different from the ones I created as long ago as thirty or even just fifteen years ago. Actually, the more recent they are the more essential and almost camouflaged. Forms and presences that are simple and dignified are not just a choice of beauty (at this age tortuous expressions do little to excite me, as I instead find a linear, serene atmosphere to be more inspiring), they guarantee that the garden will have a structure that is sufficiently flexible, as well as freedom of movement. In addition, it offers the chance to rectify any errors that, alas, often occur. The garden designer has the task of determining boundaries and indicating directions, of foreseeing and fostering changes, of favoring the life shared with animals and human beings. Tending to a garden can become a constant concern: simplicity is also the premise for a pleasant and relaxed rapport between the gardener and his plants.

When I was young I had two masters who taught me everything, but it took me a whole life to metabolize their teachings: it took project after project, experiences and assessments, many trips around the world together with the

GARDEN IN LAZIO

GARDEN IN LAZIO

International Dendrology Society and, above all, a daily familiarity with plants. Familiarity that slowly developed into knowledge and therefore insight and progressive confidence in their use.

Russell Page's projects could be very complex ones, but each and every time he made an attempt to eliminate the superfluous, to avoid useless and often banal complications. In the overall design he tended to clean up the parts that were too baroque, or excessively contorted, and as concerns the botany he offset the traditional eclecticism of mixed borders with the uniform nature of plant masses having a specific function in space. This may not be understood right away, now that his gardens are a part of history and completely different models prevail, but what they taught is more relevant than ever now, an excellent antidote to the widespread standardization of taste. Simplifying is not a question of design choices, but of method: it doesn't mean having to abandon the classical semblances of the garden in favor of unstructured and quasi-spontaneous aesthetics. Each place requires its own specific forms, and even the most solemn of parterres can be treated with dignity and discretion.

In one of the most admired places in Rome, the Teatro Marcello, I was asked to revive a small palazzo garden, encircled by high walls and with beds of centuries-old boxwood that were in a rather poor state. I decided to intervene in the lightest and most minimal way possible, from within the ancient design, replacing the boxwood plants that had been damaged, surrounding the edges with wisteria and Lady Banks roses, arranging groups of vases with pansies, petunias, lobelias, and other very common seasonal blooms inside the beds. Whether crossed by thick borders of lilies of the Nile or essential squares of *Helxine soleirolii* circling the citrus plants, as in other Roman gardens I have recently worked on, or surrounded by the dark masses of yew topiaries with an expanse of holly-leaved hellebores (*Helleborus argutifolius*), a veritable symphony of greenery that I could easily envision for a park in the Piedmont countryside (who knows whether I will ever be allowed to design one there) whether or not the garden includes botanical inventiveness, clearly even the most well-planned and artificial environments can be abreast with the times. After the elegant, composed lesson of Page came the Brazilian vitality of Roberto Burle Marx. His gardens resembled a patch of tropical forest, their forms were free and natural, and they fit in perfectly with the local vegetation and its exuberant language. The architectures vanished and the plants, repeated so as to convey a sense of uniformity, shaped the garden as if with brushstrokes. I remember Leite Garcia Park, near Petrópolis, to my mind one of his most stunning works, which I am told no longer exists, unfortunately: it consisted of penumbrae populated by moss that covered everything and replaced the grassy meadows; there was

GARDEN IN BOLGHERI

ROYAL GARDENS, VENICE

undergrowth filled with ferns, calla lilies, and gardenias, as well as soft bamboo puffballs. Gurgling water meandered from one vat to another, populated by a multicolored family of ducks. Nothing seemed to have been forced into its place—today we might call it a "fluid" garden—and the plants always looked as though they hadn't been manipulated. And just like in nature, nothing was excessively fragmentary.

Over the years I have increasingly approached the teachings of Burle Marx and the garden as something that overlooks the landscape. With other floras, no doubt, and with less sensational effects: in his works the unexpected was part and parcel of the idea, and he never gave up on strong contrasts and plot twists. It was a sort of lively botanical electric shock. However, to shock is not my priority (even though, I must confess, when it does happen I am not too displeased!) and I find the undertone very pleasing and in its own way revolutionary, whether it be the play on evergreens of the Mediterranean scrub, or the linear nature of a well-cultivated field. Although I am not at all afraid of solutions that many might find banal, I am not an advocate of the philologically correct. Mine are invented landscapes, albeit verisimilar ones: standing out amid the mastic trees of a new garden in the Argentario are the light greens of the lemon verbena (*Lippia citriodora*), and in a project on the hills of Alassio the large, soft leaves of the Mexican lilies and of the rice-paper plant harken back to the grays of the euphorbias and wild olives. All of them plants that come from the four corners of the world and that no one has ever seen grow together in nature.

I have aged a "Burle Marxian," you might say, based on my aesthetic and ethical beliefs, because that way of thinking about gardens does not just avoid rigidity in their development; it also makes them as strong and self-sufficient as possible. Burle Marx's landscapes were never self-serving, and they created careful ecosystems in which the plants supported one another, the water was carefully recycled, the soils were part of a choral reflection, the management was simplified, and the costs, including the environmental ones, diminished. This approach to sustainability, one that is very immediate and concrete, decidedly humble and not rhetorical, has become an integral part of my own work over the course of time.

Like many other gardeners, I have been witnessing the growing effects of climate change, and gradually I have tried to devise homemade remedies that would make my small world more robust and resistant. The Bramafam has changed a lot in the thirty years I have been cultivating it: woods filled with saucer magnolias have replaced old and dying chestnut trees, Lenten roses and oakleaf hydrangeas reseed themselves in all of the corners that are still moist and in the

GARDEN IN CAPRI

shade, while periwinkles have wisely and elegantly covered the dry zones. Tufts of lilies of the Nile no longer grow in vases nor protected in greenhouses during the winter; rather they grace the full earth of sunny escarpments; the *Phyllireae* have filled in all the gaps and whenever a space does open up, mock oranges, cornelian cherries, and quince trees are the candidates in pole position. Opposite the house, pink agapanthus replace annual flowers and hundreds of cuttings of *Phlomis* and holly-leaved hellebores, the offspring of my gardening frenzy during the pandemic, wait anxiously for a definitive location. The dry weather and much-discussed greenhouse effect have forced a definite shift in botanical choices, making it easier for a limited number of indefatigable species to gradually take over the space. Once again, to my mind, simplifying was the best answer.

Appropriate selections and reliable leitmotifs, besides, of course, very little water, excellent drainage systems, soil rich with life and devoid of chemicals, are the fundamental ingredients of that "liberated" garden that I still struggle to explain and practice. A garden in which woods, undergrowth, scrub, and mantles of vegetation will increasingly take the place of lawns and flower beds. Around an ancient building in the hills of Turin, which was remodeled a few years ago to host social events, I suggested nothing more than groups of trees: hundreds of Turkey oaks, holm oaks, and hazelnut trees mixed with unpruned cherry laurels, created a thick, wide, and dignified screen requiring hardly anything. Instead, in the woods of the Royal Gardens in Turin, I chose to work close to the ground and with as little visibility as possible: expanses of lilyturfs, periwinkles, barrenworts, poet's laurel (*Danae racemosa*), and other evergreen herbaceous plants that could withstand the lack of rain covered the feet of the old trunks, divided by right-angle paths. This role—now a clearly prevalent one—played by leafy species of vegetation is a sign of the times: a thick, rustic green pattern—ivy and numerous variations on the theme are unsurprisingly the key actors of my most recent works—manages to reinforce the garden, to make it take root in its place much more than a sequence of floral episodes. Also a sign of the times—and of a certain coherence that I find more and more indispensable—is the refusal to seek solutions that have an instant effect. It is extremely backward to think that a garden will immediately be pleasing: at the beginning the beauty is triggered by a correct and strong planting phase. The intrigue usually comes later, it is a result; it is the ripe fruit of good gardening and of ensuing exuberance.

For the Radicepura Garden Festival, the biennial celebration of the Mediterranean garden on the slopes of Mount Etna, we have just finished planting a small demonstrative space, a sort of prototype that I hope will succeed in summing up and conveying my thinking with immediacy and empathy. The support structure—a complex mechanism used to recycle and filter the water powered by a wind turbine and stimulated by the roots of the bulrushes, irises, ferns, and paper reeds—manifests itself without mystifications in its overt functionality. All around it we created a garden with

GARDEN OF LEAVES, CASTELLO DI RACCONIGI

GARDEN IN THE COUNTRYSIDE OF CAPALBIO

very few species (generously and newly suggested), an entire array of leaves and greens that are rather unpredictable and combined so as to achieve a great effect: arboreal and not arboreal ferns in the penumbra of the Oriental plane trees, spikenards, and multicolored reeds in the flower beds more exposed to hot weather.

Each project has its very own botany, which is more or less experimental; however, its principles are perfectly clear.

By dint of filing things down, seeking a rationale, and encouraging life, that young landscapist who looked out onto the world of plants with interest and ambition is now amazed to look back at his first garden, from when he was very young and where he grew up. A strong, discreet garden with nothing unrealistic about it, perhaps an "old Piedmont" sort of garden, with its wild strawberry borders, its flower beds of roses and peonies, and its undergrowth of violets, periwinkles, and wild cyclamens. Hence, nothing new under the sun: there is always a place in our memory that we try our entire lives to go back to. At over eighty years of age, more than a professional fulfilled by his success, more than a theoretician of the relationship between humans and nature, I feel as though I am an old manual laborer and a son of experience, a man of the trade with a very simple, earthy vision of the garden, one that is distant, very distant from ceremony and complacency.

LOCANDA ROSSA, CAPALBIO

VILLA DELLA PERGOLA, ALASSIO

The
Gardens

A Garden Whose Leaves Are Strong and Robust, but Not Enough

Garden of Leaves,
Castello di Racconigi (Turin)

Environments can speak volumes: a garden with just leaves—not endless variations, but a selection that is restricted and repeated in large groups—can become extremely captivating and remain so for a long time throughout the year. To one side of Castello di Racconigi, on a surface that in the twentieth century was set up as a tennis court, the multicolored crowns of the box elder maples offer shade to a parterre featuring sinuous, romantic shapes, the echo of the ones that were at one time suggested by Fratelli Roda. Profuse lily-of-the-valley borders encompass the abundance of plantain lilies, in varietals that all differ in dimension and color but are still perceived as being one large patchwork. Hornbeam hedges encircle the site as if it were a muffled green room, rich in light contrasts and intriguing perspectives. Easy and resistant, fed by a nearby stream, this garden could have thrived peacefully for a long time with a minimum amount of assistance, the only danger being the voracious snails there. Instead, it fell victim to neglect and no longer exists: a garden that was defunct, but fortunately, in the meantime, has been "resurrected." For some time now a cluster of peonies has been trying to capture the scene: we can only hope.

"Often, as it ages, the garden becomes shaded and it must be devoted humbly to its possible future shadows..."

A Renewed Garden

Garden in the Hills of Turin

The restoration of a historical garden can justify the use of forms that may be rather elaborate: repeating them is a way to try to save them from oblivion and to bequeath them to future generations. In this house perched in the hills of Turin, the complex system of gardens, courtyards, paths, terraces, greenhouses, and vegetable gardens was brought back to life by modernizing everything via the use of a simplified botany and one that we hope is never affected. Climbing roses drop down from the large trees in the nineteenth-century park and the Mediterranean spurges are reseeded amid the boxwoods in an Italian-style vegetable garden, to which has been added a vat to water the vegetables (it is also adored by the frogs). Plane trees shaped like parasols, wisterias, hydrangeas, and clasping-leaved twistedstalks claim the intriguing potential of a rustic courtyard; holm oaks and *Rosa chinensis* 'Sanguinea' interrupt the sun-filled gravel surfaces all around the house. Bamboo plants become precious allies to hide the borders; roses and American grapes are the leitmotifs of the pergolas; and easy annuals tone down the grassy expanses. Even the labyrinth of fruit trees cultivated as espaliers—their feet covered in tiny strawberries—proves to be less complicated than one might imagine. Directing it all is no doubt a demanding task, but each single "piece" has carved out a tiny bit more independence.

A Renewed Garden

The Garden Liberated. An Evolution of Italian Garden Design

"Growing together day after day can be very beautiful. Each beloved garden is rich in silent bonds."

A Renewed Garden

Of Shears and Imagination

Garden in the Countryside
of Capalbio (Grosseto)

On the hillside of Capalbio, surrounded by well-pruned olive trees, grows a drought-resistant garden primarily made up of shrubs. The key players here are the indigenous plants and the evergreens of the Mediterranean scrub, extrapolated from the wild and shaped into something domestic that has nothing ordinary about it, with soft, continuous shapes overlooking the landscape and sculpting the place almost mimetically. Amid the grays of the germanders and the bright greens of the narrow-leaved mock privets, in between the reddish reflections of the mastic tree and the dull green of the holm oaks and cork oaks, groups of cypresses tower over everything, bringing the scene to life. Numerous flowering presences are like seasonal bit players, smoothing over the otherwise very spare nature of the composition: lily of the Nile borders, bignonias, and Cherokee roses on the house facade, capers on the walls and, above all, untiring *Rosa chinensis* 'Sanguinea' offered here with generous abundance. Figs, pomegranates, and quinces dot the overall pattern seemingly casually, keeping alive the link with the surrounding countryside. Some citrus plants and the kumquats are given the best treatment, and the small vegetable garden is encircled by rosemary hedges. Lawns that can thrive in drought carpet the "rooms" near the house, fending off the summer's *défaillances*.

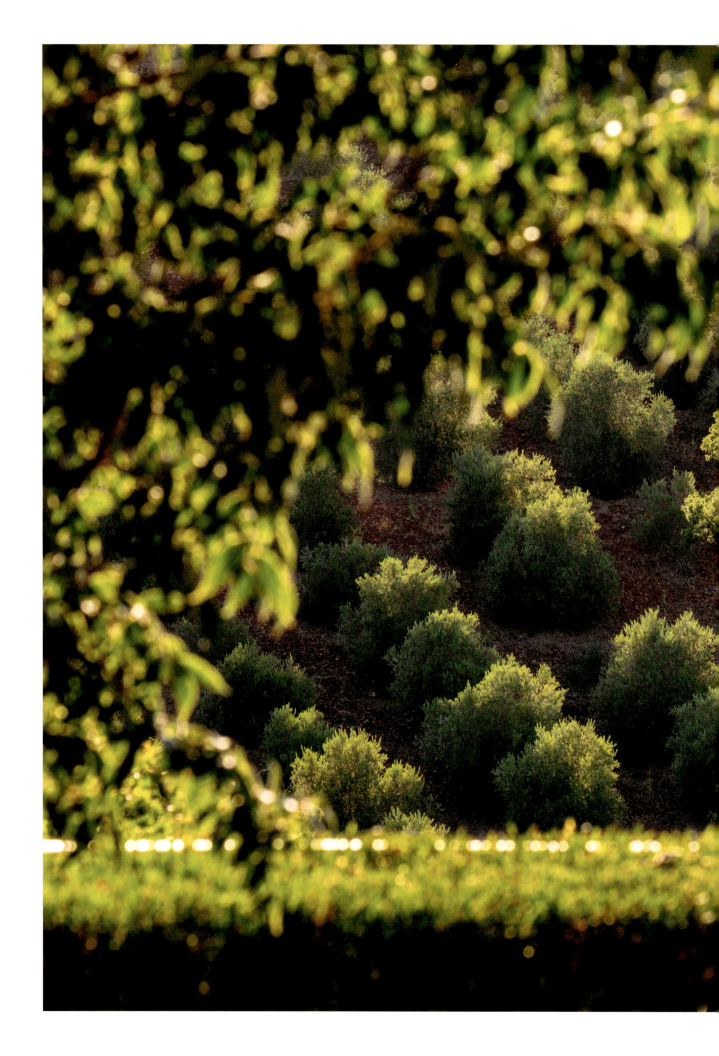

"Discreetly entering the surrounding landscape
is a form of respect toward the place.
Often the context teaches us everything."

Villa della Pergola, Alassio (Savona)

Glorious Acclimatizations from the Past and New Prospects

I believe the best effects are achieved not by congesting a garden but by singling out the right plant in the right place and letting it dominate the scene. The stunning exuberance of Villa della Pergola, in Alassio, is the result of a meticulous juxtaposition of tiers, each of which has a species that plays its own personal role to the very end. This might be the overflowing wisterias—the very ones that had already made this place famous in the days of the Hanbury—or the cascades of Lady Banks roses clinging to the cypresses, the ever-present and evergreen mantle of the climbing fig, or the glossy tangle of cycas: even a scenario as full, varied, and overwhelming as this one is based on order and simplicity. At this point the references become highly important: discovering more or less everywhere here the glossy tufts of the farfugium, the light green shades of the Boston ferns, the clamor of the lilies of the Nile, or the undertones of the poet's laurel bestows on this garden an air that is well-balanced and makes it look lived in. The design hosts some surprises as well: the gigantic fronds of the arboreal ferns, the flowered lotuses, the collection of citrus plants and succulents. Amid botanical rarities and corners of old Liguria, this rescued and liberated garden does not hesitate to show all its grateful vigor.

"Living long lives, plants grow, prosper, and age. And we with them."

Glorious Acclimatizations from the Past and New Prospects

The Garden Liberated. An Evolution of Italian Garden Design

An Ecosystem Rediscovered

Garden in Lazio

Water is the key to the success of this ancient vineyard on the broad hills of Lazio, water that is properly emphasized but always discreetly so, without futile ostentation and, more importantly, without waste. A small bambooed wood surrounds the precious spring, and thick tufts of fountain grass and Chinese silver grass skirt the gurgling brook: an unusual, rather "dry" and spartan use of grass, seeking to avoid aesthetics that are too ethereal and complacent. A rich array of swamp plants or ones that adore humidity, including gunneras, sets the scene in motion and puts the right accents on all the right places. Little by little the landscape becomes countryside, the views open up, and humidity makes way for scorching heat: climbing roses and nettle trees grow close to the farmstead, amid cobblestones cleverly brought back to life, and a well-tamed Mediterranean scrub that wraps itself around the olive trees and divides the great spaces. All the way to the vegetable garden, with its pergola of grapes and bignonias, patches for the vegetables, cut flowers, and unparalleled view of the surrounding countryside. Overlooking the garden, acres of woods have been rebuilt: holm oaks, oaks, laurustinus, and strawberry trees blend aesthetic and environmental values. It is the lively metamorphosis of a place successfully restored.

"For a garden, water is life. Plants, in their
vigorous spontaneity, are its happy counterpoint."

An Ecosystem Rediscovered

Locanda Rossa, Capalbio (Grosseto)

A Vegetable Garden with Flowers

Surrounded by a vast olive grove not far from the town of Capalbio, the Locanda Rossa is now a welcoming and picturesque fragment of Maremma. It has nothing to do with the situation we discovered upon arriving in those barren, deforested lands, orphans of their original scrub. The policy has always been the same: to dissimulate the difference from the wild and the domestic by using plant analogies and shapes that are as natural as possible. Evergreen scenery—dominated overall by mastic trees, narrow-leaved mock privets, and especially germanders—form vast clearings around a central grassy area: a rustic lawn of turkey tangle frog-fruit, which is the true heart of the place and egregiously resists the summer heat. Large hedgerows of white oleanders divide the various areas, and lots of small vegetable gardens scattered here and there benefit our eyes and aesthetic taste, contributing to upholding the rustic aspect of the whole. The cypresses play a key role, marking the roads and reinforcing the "weaker" views, and around the rooms thick curtains of plumbago and parasol-shaped mulberry trees provide guests with some privacy in the shade. A countryside that is well cadenced and well cultivated can, with just a few touches here and there, be transformed into the most pleasant of gardens.

"Rebuilding a piece of vigorous, robust, and well-laid out countryside can become the most exciting of challenges. Often more is needed."

A Vegetable Garden with Flowers

A Vegetable Garden with Flowers

An Agricultural and Happy Capri

Garden in Capri (Naples)

A garden can also nourish itself with contradictions, especially when it is located on an island as unique as Capri. A quiet and discreet Mediterranean landscape, consisting of Falanghina grape pergolas, fields of figs, parched vegetable gardens, the odd espalier of lemon plants, and small citrus groves is offset by the tropical euphoria of the flower beds and the vats situated around the pool. Palms, arboreal ferns, alocasias, dwarf and giant papyri, swamp hibiscuses, and waterlilies are deliberately redundant and alien presences here: a great amusement, an ironic *Wunderkammer* that is in its own way sustainable thanks to the calibrated reuse of the water here. Not that the "ordinary" comes without surprises: amid downy oaks and Aleppo pines, summery, puffy plumbago flowers and panicled hydrangeas revive the sober cadence of the indigenous shrubs and evergreens. Close to the house, stephanotis flowers, gardenias, and jasmines evoke distant and fragrant *clair de lunes*. The gray upon gray of a very common field of lavender at the foot of an airy olive grove remains, nonetheless, the absolute hero here: not only does it seem to expand the space and open it up toward distant and undefined views, it also bestows on the garden a center of gravity, a sort of view from inside overlooking an ancient and carefully tended agricultural territory.

"Pines, lavender, citrus plants, and olive trees, palms and water gardens: a generous oasis."

Simple and Sophisticated

Garden in Bolgheri (Livorno)

A garden that was designed on-site and most of which is made up of subtractions, the fruit of gradual and meticulous work on the pre-existing, of plants kept, moved, reunited, or gently set apart. With so much cleaning and simplifying all that is left is the essential, a skeletal structure without frills, closer to the functionality of the countryside than the flattery of the modern gardener. Clusters of germanders repeated almost obsessively form long, soft, silvery ribbons that recall the gray tones of the olive groves and separate the vineyards. Precious and well-tended vines that lie at the heart of this site's success. Once the pattern was determined, we limited ourselves to repeating it insistently, with no need for major additions: just a few escarpments of rosemary, some tufts of plumbago close to the building, and, above all, frugal buddlejes, with their ashy greens and the flowers loved by butterflies, are its principal protagonists. And how could we not have cypresses, the old and new friends of this place: we are in Bolgheri, and the famous San Guido boulevard of cypresses is just around the corner. Their dark and dense scenery surround the cultivations and make the view of what grows here more various. It is an ancient world, yet one that is abreast with the times, upheld by an approach to organic growing that is taken very seriously.

"Rigor and well-stated
moderation can serve
as a support for a wholly
special order."

Plant Minimalisms

Garden in the Hills of Bologna

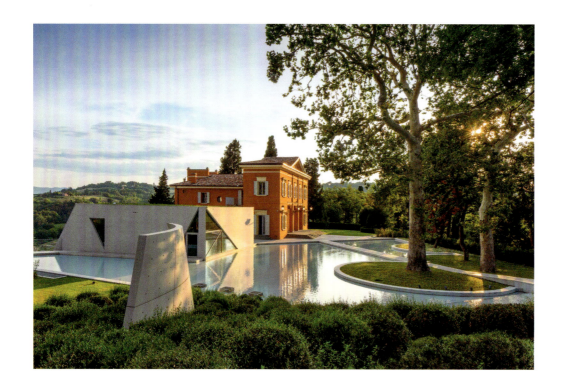

On the hills around Bologna a garden rich in contrasts was recently born. The dry and dignified architecture of Tadao Ando imposes itself next to the boxwood of the old villa and new shrubbery and herbaceous plants are already muddling its clarity. Species and varietals are certainly not unprecedented, but here they are matched curiously and unusually: patches of narrow-leaved mock privets fill the sunny surfaces and the Lady Banks roses soften the corners and straighter lines. In several areas expanses of rosemary hedges replace grassy lawns: end of February-early March is their moment of magic in the garden when their blue flowers discreetly dot the flower beds and recall the crystalline, geometric waters that lap against the buildings. Two small and transparent pools of water in pebbled containers, purposefully not "sullied" by the plants, continue this game of reflections. In the shade of some of the plane trees, circumscribed by a sort of peninsula, carpets of ivy and *Ophiopogon* spread out: this is an easy, safe, and dignified way to deal with the areas that are usually desolate at the foot of the trees. Variegated lily turfs converse quietly with the marbling of the barks. Finding company for the contemporary is often one of the toughest challenges for the landscapist.

"Sometimes beauty is due to simplicity:
too many complications and too many
sophisticated elaborations can make us lose
sight of the key to unlocking the problem..."

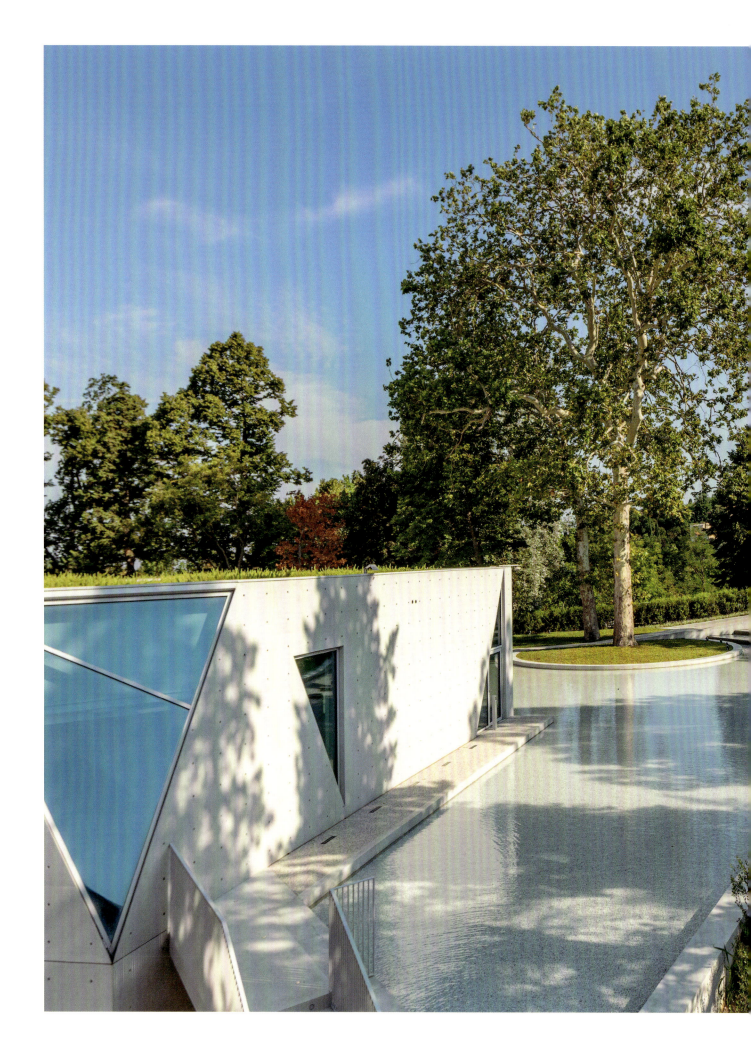

Colle dell'Infinito, Recanati (Macerata)

Repairs

A garden that is not a garden, where the intervention of the landscapist is as rarefied as possible and becomes a sort of meticulous repair work careful to preserve and exalt the consolidated ambience. The Colle dell'Infinito, in Recanati, certainly needs no celebration, decoration, or (worse yet) reinvention: the small rustic and destructured vegetable gardens—an absolute triumph of the ephemeral—,the long pergolas of vines, bignonias, and roses, the old fruit trees, all of them somewhat crooked, seemed to me the most concrete and genuine way to approach a place as filled with meaning as this one is. Precisely like the dense groups of cypresses, the corners of the Mediterranean scrub, the climbing roses on the facades, or the mixed borders filled with aromatic herbs and flowers for cutting that smack of the antique and the peasant-like. Beyond the famous hedge described by the great Italian poet Giacomo Leopardi, down there at the very end of the embankment: nothing less apparent and more quietly stated. Hence, no strong connotation, no search for uniformity: in this case the story of the place as well as its composite and fragmented character prevail. The project was not meant to overlap anything here, and it also avoided any signs of museumification: the Colle remains a place that is alive and kicking, rustic and enthralling.

"A sober, domestic garden, and above all one that is free from preconceived plans to exalt Leopardi's Solitary Hill, its harmonious silence, and its discretion."

A Lagoonal Triumph

Royal Gardens, Venice

Why not reinterpret the grandiosity of the Italian-style garden in a contemporary key? That is what we tried to do in Venice, maintaining unchanged the forms and cadences, but "exploding them" through an abundance of flora never seen before. Hydrangeas, farfugias, spikenards, and, above all, lilies of the Nile reinvented the parterres of the Royal Gardens, transforming them into broad waves of plant life that conquer the space here: showy blooms in season create precise, and by now eagerly awaited, appointments, but the leaves are the real protagonists in this scenario that is anything but indigenous and upheld by a cosmopolitan rationale. The result manages to be both harmonious and clearly heterogeneous. Small woods filled with sophoras and Caucasian wingnut trees guarantee quick and exotic shadows, defining a catalog of species that can resist the northerly winds and the saline humidity. Even the gigantic vases filled with fruit plants typical of the Mediterranean garden are part of the attempt to actualize and they constitute a type of overview for visitors of the not-always-negative consequences of the greenhouse effect. The real eye-catcher, however, is the long cast-iron pergola covered with wisteria and pink podranea: a garden that welcomes guests and is capable of transmitting new ideas.

"An ensemble of memories and fresh ideas for a fascinating place, rich with leaves and scents."

A Lagoonal Triumph

Whether Indigenous or Not, Cultivating and Testing Are Part and Parcel of the Game

Whether Indigenous or Not, Cultivating
and Testing Are Part and Parcel of the Game

**A Garden Whose Leaves Are Strong
and Robust, but Not Enough
Garden of Leaves**
Castello di Racconigi (Turin)

Acer negundo "Variegatum"

Carpinus betulus

Hosta varieties

Ophiopogon japonicus

A Renewed Garden
Garden in the Hills of Turin

Acanthus mollis

Buxus sempervirens

Camellia japonica

Carpinus betulus

Euphorbia characias

Ficus pumila

Fragaria vesca

Helleborus orientalis

Hydrangea macrophylla varieties

Hydrangea quercifolia

Phyllostachys mitis

Platanus orientalis

Quercus ilex

Rosa "Cooper's Burmese"

Rosa "Hot Cocoa"

Rosa "Iceberg"

Rosa "Just Joey"

Rosa "Madame Alfred Carrière"

Rosa "Paul Transon"

Rosa bracteata

Rosa chinensis "Sanguinea"

Rosa filipes "Kiftsgate"

Rosa moschata "Paul's Himalayan Musk"

Ruscus racemosus

Vitis labrusca (fox grape)

Wisteria sinensis

Of Shears and Imagination
Garden in the Countryside
of Capalbio (Grosseto)

Agapanthus africanus

Celtis australis

Citrus japonica

Citrus x aurantium

Cupressus sempervirens

Cydonia oblonga

Eriobotrya japonica

Ficus carica

Ficus pumila

Laurus nobilis

Myrtus communis subsp. *tarentina*

Narcissus jonquilla

Olea europaea

Phillyrea angustifolia

Pistacia lentiscus

Prunus armeniaca

Punica granatum

Quercus ilex

Quercus suber

Rosa "Albéric Barbier"

Rosa bracteata

Rosa chinensis "Sanguinea"

Rosa laevigata

Rosmarinus officinalis

Teucrium fruticans

Wisteria floribunda "Longissima Alba"

**Glorious Acclimatizations from
the Past and New Prospects**
Villa della Pergola, Alassio (Savona)

Agapanthus in a collection

Asparagus densiflorus "Meyeri"

Asparagus densiflorus "Sprengeri"

Beschorneria yuccoides

Bougainvillea spectabilis

Campsis grandiflora

Citrus in a collection

Clivia miniata

Cyathea cooperi

Cycas in a collection

Dahlia imperialis

Distictis buccinatoria

Echium fastuosum

Erythrina crista-galli

Farfugium japonicum

Ficus pumila

Heliotropium arborescens

Lonicera hildebrandiana

Nelumbo nucifera

Nephrolepis cordifolia

Podranea ricasoliana "Contessa Sara"

Rosa banksiae

Ruscus hypoglossum

Ruscus racemosus

Tetrapanax papyrifer

Wisteria (in a collection of 34 varieties)

An Ecosystem Rediscovered
Garden in Lazio

Acer campestre
Arbutus unedo
Campsis grandiflora
Campsis x tagliabuana "Madame Galen"
Celtis australis
Crataegus monogyna
Ginkgo biloba
Gunnera manicata
Hedera helix
Hydrangea arborescens "Annabelle"
Iris pseudacorus
Liriodendron tulipifera
Lythrum salicaria
Miscanthus sinensis "Gracillimus"
Miscanthus sinensis "Zebrinus"
Myrtus communis
Nerium oleander
Parrotia persica
Pennisetum alopecuroides
Phyllostachys mitis
Populus alba
Prunus spinosa
Prunus subhirtella
Punica granatum
Pyracantha "Navaho"
Quercus frainetto
Quercus robur
Rosa "Burgundy Iceberg"
Rosa "Clair Matin"
Rosa "Mermaid"
Rosa palustris
Sorbus domestica
Spartium junceum
Viburnum tinus

A Vegetable Garden with Flowers
Locanda Rossa, Capalbio (Grosseto)

Campsis x tagliabuana "Madame Galen"
Cupressus sempervirens
Fragaria vesca
Lippia nodiflora
Morus platanifolia "Fruitless"
Nerium oleander
Olea europaea
Pelargonium zonale
Phillyrea angustifolia
Pistacia lentiscus
Plumbago auriculata
Punica granatum
Quercus ilex
Quercus pubescens
Rosa "Albéric Barbier"
Rosa chinensis "Sanguinea"
Teucrium fruticans
Tilia tomentosa
Tropaeolum majus

An Agricultural and Happy Capri
Garden in Capri (Naples)

Alocasia sp.
Arecastrum romanzoffianum
Asparagus densiflorus "Meyeri"
Cyrtomium falcatum
Dicksonia antarctica
Ficus carica
Gardenia jasminoides
Hibiscus moscheutos
Hydrangea paniculata
Lavandula angustifolia
Olea europaea
Osmunda regalis
Phillyrea angustifolia
Phoenix reclinata
Plumbago auriculata
Quercus pubescens
Rhapis excelsa
Stephanotis
Teucrium fruticans
Thalia dealbata
Victoria amazonica

Simple and Sophisticated
Garden in Bolgheri (Livorno)

Buddleja davidii

Cupressus sempervirens

Olea europaea

Plumbago auriculata

Rosmarinus officinalis

Teucrium fruticans

Plant Minimalisms
Garden in the Hills of Bologna

Capparis spinosa

Cornus sanguinea

Hedera helix

Iris foetidissima

Liriope spicata "Silver Dragon"

Ophiopogon japonicus "Kyoto"

Parrotia persica

Phillyrea angustifolia

Quercus ilex

Rosa banksiae "Purezza"

Rosmarinus officinalis "Boule"

Ruscus racemosus

Viburnum tinus

Vinca major

Repairs
Colle dell'Infinito, Recanati (Macerata)

Agapanthus africanus

Aloysia citriodora

Aspidistra elatior

Cosmos bipinnatus

Cupressus sempervirens

Dahlia

Dianthus "Kahori"

Erigeron karvinskianus

Hosta plantaginea

Iris dalmatica

Iris florentina

Jasminum humile "Revolutum"

Jasminum nudiflorum

Laurus nobilis

Lilium candidum

Myrtus communis

Narcissus poeticus

Paeonia lactiflora "Duchesse de Nemours"

Phillyrea angustifolia

Pistacia lentiscus

Rosa banksiae

Rosa bracteata

Salvia microphylla

Salvia sclarea

Tulbaghia violacea

Vitis labrusca

Wisteria sinensis

Ziziphus jujuba

A Lagoonal Triumph
Royal Gardens, Venice

Agapanthus "Queen Mum"

Agapanthus africanus

Cinnamomum camphora

Citrus x aurantium

Clerodendrum trichotomum

Eriobotrya japonica

Farfugium japonicum

Ficus carica

Hedera helix

Hydrangea arborescens "Annabelle"

Hydrangea paniculata "Kyushu"

Iris dalmatica

Iris florentina

Liriope muscari

Myrtus communis

Osmanthus fragrans

Phyllostachys metake

Phyllostachys viridiglaucescens

Pistacia lentiscus

Plumbago auriculata

Podranea ricasoliana "Contessa Sara"

Pterocarya fraxinifolia

Punica granatum

Rosa "Général Schablikine"

Ruscus racemosus

Sophora japonica

Tetrapanax papyrifer

Viburnum lucidum

Wisteria floribunda "Black Dragon"

Wisteria sinensis

Editorial Project Manager
Valentina Lindon

Graphic Design
olgastudio.it

Translation by
Sylvia Adrian Notini

Heartfelt thanks are due to all those who either directly or indirectly collaborated on the creation of some of these gardens. In particular, I wish to express my gratitude to Architetto Franco Brugo and with him to Paola and Silvia, to Alberto Fusari, to the gardeners Giuseppe Dionisi, Silvio Armando, Niccolò and Fiorella Degl'Innocenti, and Andrea De Zottis.

© 2023 Mondadori Libri S.p.A.
Distributed in English throughout the World
by Rizzoli International Publications Inc.
300 Park Avenue South
New York, NY 10010, USA

ISBN: 978-88-918405-5-4

2023 2024 2025 2026 / 10 9 8 7 6 5 4 3 2 1

First edition: March 2024

All rights reserved. No part of this publication may be reproduced, stored in a retrieval system, or transmitted in any form or by any means, electronic, mechanical, photocopying, recording, or otherwise, without prior consent of the publishers.

This volume was printed at L.E.G.O. S.p.A., Vicenza
Printed in Italy

Visit us online:
Facebook.com/RizzoliNewYork
Twitter: @Rizzoli_Books
Instagram.com/RizzoliBooks
Pinterest.com/RizzoliBooks
Youtube.com/user/RizzoliNY
Issuu.com/Rizzoli